Author's Note

I feel so blessed to have been given a tremendous amount of support and encouragement from my family and friends throughout my journey in writing this book. I am honored to dedicate these poems to God and our savior Jesus Christ, also to the many people who are looking for some inspiration and a little reminder; we are never alone in this world. Every one of us has a gift of some sort that he has given us to make a difference on this earth. They may be as big as being a leader of the church that is spreading his word, to small acts of kindness that can change someone's life for the better and lead them to-wards being a stronger believer. It only takes the size of a mustard seed of faith to be guided into heaven. There is going to be a constant war in our souls because our culture is in serious chaos. If we all could see the big picture drawn for us and truly give wounded hearts and broken hope to God, he has the power to mend them. I hope and pray these words help others as much as they have helped me. I am eternally grateful for the holy spirit that has lead me towards this gift and is helping me share these words with you. The bible is a beautiful love story and I feel so honored to be able to share some of it with you.

A special thank you to my brother Brent who helped me edit this book. I couldn't have done this without him.

Then you will call
on me and come and pray
to me, and I will listen to
you. You will seek me and
find me when you
seek me with
all your
.heart.

Jeremiah 29: 12-13

Presented to:

_____

From:

_____

Date:

_____

Treasured Hearts

by **Stephanie Traina**

Contents

Faith Within Him

The beauty in believing Jesus is truly here
makes everything easier without fear. Hold
on to his love with all of your heart because his
words will keep you from falling apart. There
will be days when the evil of this world will
try to tear you far from his vision but he has
your path made up with passionate precision.
Keep your faith and trust within and he will
help you get through the thick and thin.
Letting go of your past mistakes; praying for
forgiveness is all it takes. He knows all of
your sorrows and pain. One day they will be
gone and God's kingdom we will gain. Try
your hardest to be patient and kind because
when you do, you'll never be left behind. So
keep the strength to overcome and there will
be so much more freedom. When meeting
Jesus and seeing his graceful face, he will be
showing loving arms with a glorious embrace.

for Nina

This is love: not that we

loved God, but that he loved us

and sent his Son as an atoning

sacrifice for our sins.

1 John 4:10

He is in Control

When I have moments of despair, I then
realize you have my mind under repair.
Thank you for pointing me in the right
direction by keeping my heart in your
protection. Sometimes I don't put you as
my main desire but inside I know I need
to put you higher. Seeing you make
changes in me takes away my thoughts
of controversy. I know when I am craving
the truth, looking to the bible is your holy
proof. My selfish ways I will sacrifice and
use your words as my spiritual device. I'm
trying to show a gracious recovery while
understanding my soul is under discovery.
I will have faith in all your promises because I know I'm not rejected, but accept-
ed. You are in my life; rain or shine,
now all your love I will see as mine.

In the past God overlooked

such ignorance, but now

he commands all people

everywhere to repent.

Acts 17:30

One Day

Jesus says to be patient and kind and when
we don't try to be, we get lost in our mind.
Breaking the rules throughout our day, re-
grettably there will be prices to pay. When
we think we can do this on our own, for-
getfulness is sadly shown. Looking back
on the heartaches and pain, some depress-
ingly think he is to blame. Try to realize
everything happens for a reason and that
it is not torturous treason. So get to know
him as soon as possible and see it is surely
plausible. Eternal love is what he will forever give, now let's show him the right
way to live. Believe one day we will see
his face, he then will share his forgiv-
ing grace. Gratefulness is what he deserves, just please see that you can trust
he has seats in heaven for you reserved.

Do not let your heart be

troubled. You believe in God;

believe also in me.

John 14:1

Graceful

Believing in God's beautiful kingdom,
means you will have eternal freedom.
Look around and try to embrace, this world
can be full of grace. Proving he is our one
true king, our hearts full of love we should
proudly bring. To present a positive example,
try sharing loving arms for a sample. These
good works are in definite need, that is why
they should be in the lead. When there are
days you feel those thoughts of fear, God
does not want us to shed a tear. Praying for
Jesus to show us the right way to live means
we need to pour out our hearts to forgive.
Give him all your glorious smiles, then you
will be able to walk many gracious miles.
When you truly promise your heart, in time,
you will have reached your holy prime.
Just realize we are works of art and we will
be finished when we do our final part.

But to each one of us grace

has been given as Christ

apportioned it.

Ephesians 4:7

Staying Strong

The loss of a loved one can be so heart-wrenching to go through, but holding on to their memory will be forever true. You won't ever forget the way they smiled or what they were like as a child. Dreams of them will come and go; their presence they will sometimes show. We will always keep them in our hearts until the end of our time; seeing them waiting for us on the other side in their prime.

The Lord is close to the broken-
hearted and saves those who
are crushed in spirit.

Psalm 34:18

Okay With It

I was scared to be bipolar but then I found
you again, proving it was not my controller.
Having so many thoughts that were not
mine; I didn't realize it was a sign. Day by
day they slowly crept and it was something
I had to accept. I have been given the strength to overcome, it has given me so much
more freedom. This is where I will let go of
that shame so my heart will no longer have that
strain. Thank you, God, for showing your
amazing support; your love I shall never abort.

Here is a trustworthy saying that deserves full acceptance: Christ Jesus came into the world to save sinners- of whom I am the worst.

1 Timothy 1:15

Sunrise

Waking up in the morning is a blessing in disguise and one day we will realize how it has been a wonderful prize. Showing God how grateful we are is to keep our minds from going afar. He is our beginning and our end, that is why his honor we need to always defend. There are miracles given by him every day so we should present our hearts so they don't stray. Jesus gave his life for us, now let's all take a ride on his glorious bus. He has shown all the beauty along the way, we will forever get the privilege to pray.

Then celebrate the Festival of

Weeks to the LORD your God by

giving a freewill offering in

proportion to the blessings the

LORD your God has given you.

Deuteronomy 16:10

Passionate Love

When you stare into my eyes, I know your
love is astonishingly true; seeing how there is
a tremendous amount you will help get me
through. I'm not always the person you want
me to be, but I know that no matter what, you
will have my back and never flee. I am going
to love you for the rest of my days and this is
only our beginning phase. I am truly proud
of the man you have become, especially from
the situation you came from. You show me
you are a loving father also to your only
daughter. Our boys have for you so much
adoring pride and will follow your encourag-
ing ways in stride. Proving that there is nothing you can't do makes me significantly
appreciate how you have made us a special
crew. Never backing down from anything
that comes our way, for you my love,
your safety I will forever pray.

for Ryan

15

Wives, submit yourselves to your

husbands, as is fitting in the Lord.

Husbands, love your wives and

do not be harsh with them.

Colossians **3:18-19**

Bundles of Joy

While I stand in our hallway and look up at
our family pictures, there are so many happy
smiles with precious cures. Reflecting on all
the places we have been, I feel so blessed they
are my children. Starting to walk passed our
boys' room, I think how I treasured them when
they were in my womb. I see all the books we
have read, while thinking about the prayers
we have said. They have great pride in all
their love for the Lord and how we are sharing as much love we can afford. Wondering
about what will be the next steps in their lives,
I hope they will still have that faith in Jesus
and they pray that it thrives. I thank God for
the amazing life he has given us; we all have
many more plans to discuss. Such beautiful
boys they have come to be that I am truly
proud to say good men we will see.

for Chase and Cole

Children are a heritage

from the Lord, offspring

a reward from him.

Psalm 127:3

Once Away

Sometimes I feel like a stranger with all of this unwanted anger. This bipolar medicine takes memories away that I pray could stay. These days go along, with me trying to be strong. I know not to have shame because I am not to blame. I am not alone, seeing they can be just like me. I hate to be mean when all I want to be is gleam. I feel God wouldn't have given me the name if I could not handle this strain. I felt so lost in translation, but knowing now it was my mind on a vacation. Thank you for saving me from the direction I was headed and helping me see it was one I would have dreaded. I understand my new life, and will try my hardest to be a loving mother and wife.

Guard my life and rescue me;

do not let me be put to shame,

for I take refuge in you.

Psalm 25:20

Unfailing Love

Walking up to her grave, my pounding heart
not feeling completely brave. There were tears
falling down my broken face, hoping to feel his
holy grace. How I wished so badly that I could
have met this beautiful golden blonde little girl,
with her bright smile as shiny as a glorious
pearl. She had so much adoring giving love, I
prayed I could have been a part of. There was a
tremendous amount of pain in my defeated
soul, that felt like it was filled with undesired
coal. A red dragonfly flew on the decorative
hanging bar with me wondering if it was her
showing me support from afar. There was
powerful doubt that lied in my tangled mind,
thinking it was not something I would find.
After a short while, she also sent a white
butterfly that landed on the bar to show it was
her with no denial. My shattered dreams of the
person I wanted to be, she was showing reassu-
ance that "happy" somebody was still in me.
From then on I knew everything would be okay
because for her protection I would forever pray.
One day I will get the chance to see, her step-
mom I will have the privilege to be.

for Brooklynne

"Oh, that I might have my

request, that God would grant

what I hope for."

Job 6:8

Answered Prayers

Jesus, please help me keep my thoughts
from going astray. Being with you is what
I pray. Thank you for letting me be a mother and wife, you have given me a incredibly
wonderful life. I will try to show you all
of my love and look for your signs given
from above. You will always be my one true
king, for you, my heart I will gladly bring.
I am so grateful to be blessed with all my
family and friends. You are always showing many promising amends. In you are
the joys that are truly amazing; you are
the one I will forever be praising.

Amen

All these blessings will come

on you and accompany you if

you obey the lord your God.

Deuteronomy 28:2

Humbled

You bring so much joy to my life by
giving me the chance to be a mother and
wife. I see you in every moment they smile,
all of this work is so worth while. I want
them to look into my eyes and see you, knowing your holy grace is so true. Lord, you are
the one who meets my deepest needs, so I
am going to try my hardest to do my holy
deeds. Please help me use my words to share
your love and for them to acknowledge it is
truly you from above. There are times I know
will be hard to abide but it makes everything easier having you by my side.

my boys'

So do not Fear, for I am with you;

do not be dismayed, for I am

your God. I will strengthen you;

I will uphold you with my

righteous right hand.

Isaiah 41:10

My Trust Within

I will write for you forever and it will
continuously be my endeavor. Praying to
stay strong for the rest of my days, I am
going to show you all my praise. Looking
up into the skies is where I will find you;
the hard times I know you will get me
through. So many blessings you are displaying to me every day. I am eternally grateful, for you, I will always pray. I can sometimes hear you send messages through a song,
it becomes my medicine, so unimaginably
strong. Thank you for what you have given
me. With you is where my heart will graciously be. Spreading your words wherever I go,
please help me say the right things so
through me you will peacefully show.

Trust in the Lord with all your

heart and lean not on your own

understanding; in all your ways

submit to him, and he will

make your paths straight.

Proverbs 3:5-6

Winner's Circle

Having reassurance he is gracefully
walking by my side helps me keep my
thoughts to proudly abide. His astonishing
ways make everything easier to do, the
guidance shown is so shockingly true.
Trying to notice the signs being displayed
throughout my day, those precious
moments will stick like clay. All the crazy
situations I may not always want to be
part of, are sent with an appreciative test
from above. I want to show people all the
kindness I can give, so hopefully they might
see the right way to live. Praying to change
someone's day into a better one, I then
realize God's work is gladly being done.

Whatever you do, work at it with

all your heart, as working for

the Lord, not for human masters.

Colossians 3:23

His Love

I need to stand apart from the crowd and
show them having you in my life makes me
so proud. So many doubts I had about you,
but you've lead my soul in believing you are
forever true. There were times I would think
you were not with me but, by my side, you
say you will always be. Guiding me to get
through all my struggles and pain, you are
rewiring the thoughts within my brain. I pray
to repent for all of my sins because I know
there will be many spiritual amends. I now
have confidence in pursuing you as much as
I can, and will try to understand that for me,
you have a plan. Taking the next step head-
ing to your promising words, you are helping
me from moving backwards. Lord, you have
shown me so much faithfulness; I know it
will be something I will forever witness.

Let the wise listen and add to

their learning, and let the

discerning get guidance.

Proverbs 1:5

Beautiful Soul

Staring down the hallway at this broken
girl with tears in her eyes, my thoughts
were, "oh no, is it her family that is the
reason she cries?" They do not know what
they are truly blessed with, a person that
everybody loves to be with. The astonishing advice she gives is so very wise and
some days she will even bring you a
thoughtful surprise. Her heart is always
bursting with love, I am so honored I will
have the privilege to be a part of. She
never says you are not worth her time or
that she will not help you up that moun-
tain you have to climb. A friend to every-
one she unfailingly tries to be and just know
she is forever going to have a shoulder to
cry on for you and me. Her strength in this
life is what I strive for. I hope and pray we
will always have this connection forever
more. I'm going to love her until the day I
die, and will see that no matter what
happens she won't ever say goodbye.

for Christine

Perfume and incense bring joy

to the heart, and the pleasant-

ness of a friend springs from

their heartfelt advise.

Proverbs 27:9

His Vision

In every experience you have with
another person, pray to Jesus for it to be
an eye opening excursion. So much you
can learn about life from one another on
this earth, and see how precious our hearts
are worth. Realize every moment we have
with each other could be our last, and to let
go of that haunting anger from the past.
Your regret can be extremely crippling if
you let it, but don't accept that it can
destroy your spirit. He is not done with us
yet, so show him you will no longer fret.
He is providing us with his glorious
presents by sharing the circle of life with
his cosmic essence. Reaching out to be a
best friend, he can give you a spiritual
mend. Try to appreciate the time he is
giving us here and now because when we
see him we will be taking a gracious bow.

And we know that in all things

God works for the good of those

who love him, who have been

called according to his purpose.

Romans 8:28

His Knocking

The Devil will try to put a lock on your heart but God knows the code and will do his part. Without his love our souls would be lost forever, so we need to look to him as our never ending endeavor. When there are those haunting regrets and fears, pray for him to take away your heart-breaking tears. Sometimes we have to lose it all to find our way, and trust in him to give us a new day. We should show that our faith in him we do not lack because he will forever have our back. Jesus loves us more then we can comprehend, so accept that he truly is our friend. This is the time to watch and be alert because the day he is coming will take away the hurt. Don't be naive, and see how there is a shocking amount of trust in this you can achieve. Now we have to get our priorities straight so that we don't have a horrible fate. Believe when it comes our way with tremendous force, it is going to set our heavenly course. Live dangerously for his namesake because our hearts he is going to graciously take. Now is the time to surrender to the the kingdom of God, and join his holy squad. So let's dance for him with our gracious feet, and move to the Jesus beat.

And now, dear children,

continue in him, so that when

he appears we may be

confident and unashamed

before him at his coming.

1 John 2:28

Inhale...Exhale

Time tells all truth inside and out; sometimes all I want to do is angrily shout. It is an unwanted feeling to try to hide this bipolar stigma with pride. That me I used to be cries out with a huge plea. I can make this shame go away, with my emotions I will surly pay. Normal is what I want to be but that is something people don't always see. I am tired of feeling locked up in this cage, filled with uncontrollable rage. There is always trauma that comes with this drama. I don't want to feel all this spite come out of me unexpectedly. These episodes come and go, sadly I am starting to feel like a pro. Praying to take over this disbelief within me, graceful is what I want to be.

When Jesus saw their faith,

he said, "Friend, your

sins are forgiven."

Luke 5:20

Strength of This Mama

Thinking about all of the hurdles of what
will come next, she enjoys her little one's when
they give her precious pecks. Having all the
weight of their worlds on top of her shoulders,
she walks proudly when thinking about her
words being their molders. Amazingly she can
do this mostly on her own, being a mother of
three presents her strength in this life that is
surly being shown. She has started with the
double duty of twin boys that are very ramb-
unctious and sweet, and has added a beautiful
baby girl that doesn't miss a beat. She doesn't
realize what she is doing is a blessing in disguise; those babies are a wonderful prize.
Thankfulness is what one day she will receive
because her respect from them she will
achieve. She is praying for her heart to stay
strong, believing her teachings will never be
wrong. So proud I am to call her my friend;
her wise words she will forever lend.

for Krislyn

41

A friend loves at all times,

and a brother is born for

a time in adversity.

Proverbs 17:17

Getting Together

Having planned this summer barbecue
with family and friends, I'm looking around
and seeing a beautiful amount of blends.
Thinking about how every time we get to-
gether, I see how there are so many laughs
with each other. Realizing our household is
the glue that keeps our whole family connec-
ted, we see how much it makes our happy
hearts loved and respected. All of the stories
that are being told around the fire are making
our thoughts about one another even higher.
I love sharing our home with all our loved
ones, praying there will be many more reruns.
Thank you, Jesus, for sharing your vision
and for pointing us in the right direction.

You will eat the fruit of

your labor; blessings and

prosperity will be yours.

Psalm 128:2

Truthful Words

When you feel like falling into pieces,
all you need to do is give your worries
to Jesus. He understands how you feel
because his undeserved crucifixion was
truly real. There isn't a day he is not with
you and nothing he can't get you through.
Sometimes it is easy to forget he is by your
side but both your hearts will forever coll-
ide. When you search for your faith within
him, just trust he will get you through the
thick and thin. When you feel lost, he says
he will show you the direction by forever
keeping your soul under his protection.

If my people, who are called by

my name, will humble themselves

and pray and seek my face and

turn from their wicked ways,

then I will hear from heaven,

and I will forgive their sin and

will heal their land.

2 Chronicles 7:14

The Hard Walk

The truth can be a scary thing to accept
because sometimes it will help you keep
promises you have kept but other times it can
bring you shame, or even push you to blame.
When you're stuck in the middle of a cross-
road, and don't know which way to take, have
faith in Jesus that he is going to point you in
the right direction he will make. You can
choose to step forward towards the easy way
through, or show you are stronger and follow
what is really true. When trying to decide the
right decision by listening to your heart, unfor-
tunately, the struggles of this life can tear them
apart. Don't let them take over your destiny
already made, which he has given with the
prices he paid. We can't let the crudeness of
this world pull us away from his voice so look
around for the signs he is showing you to make
the right choice. No matter how hard dealing
with the consequences are, the glory of God's
kingdom will not be very far. For our minds to
be in an honorable place, we must take the path
with dignity and grace. So stand proud for
doing what's right. God will protect your
righteous soul with all of his might.

for Ron

47

I can do all this through

him who gives me strength.

Philippians 4:13

Our Praise

Living a christian life isn't always the
easiest thing to do because being faithful
to his words can be an indescribable
issue. People don't always pray to repent
and others feel it is a depressing discourage-
ment. There are ways to have faith in his
glory; all you need to do is believe in his
story. He is our one true king so our souls
we need to proudly bring. The truth is powerful about this place. It is not always filled
with glorious grace. Evil is all around us
everyday, now what we should do is kneel
down and pray. When you feel that empti-
ness inside your heart, believe that letting
him in can be a new start. Jesus does not
want us to feel sorrow because he will
forever give us a new tomorrow.

If we confess our sins, he is

faithful and just to forgive us

our sins, and purify us from

all unrighteousness.

1 John 1:9

Acceptance

There is so much religious division with such
heartless precision. Many have forgotten how
to believe, and have started to deceive. God
is showing that this world can't be lived in
without his glorious discipline. We need to
pray to escape these meaningless expecta-
tions, and hope there is peace with all nations.
Every person has to let go of their selfish-
ness, and show so much more selflessness.
Time in this world is so much shorter than
we think because the end of days are surely
on the brink; signs are being displayed
around the earth and ultimately there will be
a holy re-birth. As long as you are committ-
ed to his heart, he will never keep you apart.
We have to practice his love and rejoice
because we have the ultimate choice. If we
can endure the struggles of this place, and do
our best not to offend, our hearts Jesus will
forever defend. One day there will be no more
pain and heaven we will graciously gain.

Therefore keep watch,

because you do not know on

what day your Lord will come.

Matthew 24:42

Pathway to Heaven

Society wants us all to attempt being perfect but instead we should see the side
effect. There are days when our minds will
be hazy, even feeling like we are going
crazy. Some think being at the top is to feel
alive but Jesus tells us it is not something to
strive. He instructs us to live in his image
and that it is an amazing privilege. God's
paradise is our one true home, and when we
accept that, we will never be alone. By choos-
ing him first, you will never be wrong because it is where our hearts belong. It is time
to make praying an intention and not for it to
be an objection. There is so much beauty in his
loving arms so let them be our blessed alarms.

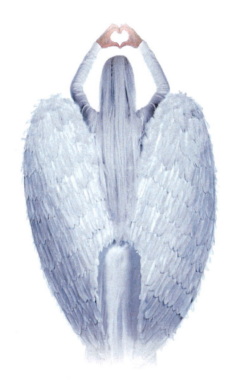

For lack of guidance a nation

falls, but victory is won

through many advisers.

Proverbs 11:14

No More Worries

Having fear can be so paralyzing so letting go of it is something we should be realizing. Don't let it take your faith in him away because it will brake your beloved heart one day. Try getting through the battle inside, when you do, it will truly be easier to abide. He is showing you how you have been reborn and that in the end you will never again have to mourn. Now show him your love with all of your heart so your soul will never fall apart. He is rescuing you from all of your struggles and pain; you are going to see how much trust in him you will gain. Even if your voice is out of key, keep singing for him to be set free.

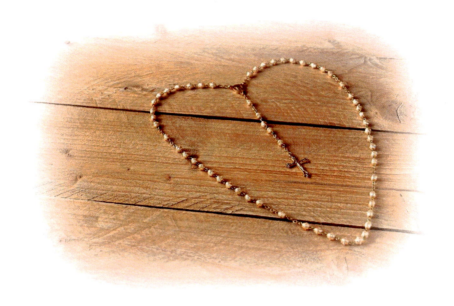

But these are written that you

may believe that Jesus is the

Messiah, the Son of God, and

that by believing you may

have life in his name.

John 20:31

With You

I hear you calling my soul day by day and I am so grateful; I will forever pray. Thank you for sending the holy spirit to speak to me so I can help give hope to the hopeless, and make you their main focus. The strength of your love is showing that you are the glorious one from above. Many believe you are not there, oh how much I want to tell them that is not fair. You are displaying to us the grace you are giving but some try to tell themselves it's just the life they are living. People are constantly saying that it is just luck on their side but they truly need to let go of that pride. God, you are bringing so many blessings in disguise. If only they believed in them, they would be so impressively wise. Grateful is what we should be but instead we don't always thank thee. Beautifulness are the times to come, hopefully they will have the vision of where we came from. In the end we will all see being with you is where we want to be.

"The one who sent me is with me;

He has not left me alone, for I

always do what pleases him."

John 8:29

Never Giving Up

The enemy will always try to push you off
track, but just know we travel in a huge pack.
There is a glorious army of hearts and prayers
to which have many layers. All you have to do
is close your eyes and say Jesus' name, then in
that moment he will take away your shame.
This world can drag us down by making
many unexpected struggles; what we should
do is give him our strenuous troubles. Open
your eyes and wake up to realize that we are
not bullet proof and he is going to always
present us with the full truth. We need to keep
searching for God non-stop and that will put
us back at the top. So give thanks to the one
who shows you unconditional love and he
will forever give you a spiritual shove.

Listen to advice and accept

discipline, and at the end you

will be counted among the wise.

Proverbs 19:20

Hope for Humanity

Lord, please rid us of our selfish ways and at
the end of our days let us give you gracious
praise. We want to truly be free so help us
please see the one's you need us to be,
Yahweh. In this time of scary belief, what
we want is a release but what we truly need
is peace. God, we keep moving through the
motions like the oceans and the potions of
this little thing we we'd like to call life. We
believe we know how to live on our own but,
Jesus, you know the truth because you are
the living proof. I can't understand how I
didn't see the real me, the one you need me
to be for you and them now. Father, please
show them how all the killings and the
billings of this life are for now, not forever
like we think, but only temporary. Jehovah,
we are all your children and you are our
true love; the one looking down from
above on us now so how can't we see we
need thee, your never ending love is to be
free. Our healing is in your hands now let us
be your bands. All we want is to be redeemed
and not something that is only dreamed.

Your right hand, LORD,

was majestic in power.

Your right hand, LORD,

shattered the enemy.

Exodus 15:6

Her Gift From Above

Having just read our book and said our prayers,
asking Jesus to watch over us with all his cares.
We end them with "God bless Brooklynne and
Kine in heaven and everybody else in the world",
soon after closing their eyes into the dreamworld.
I laid down with many thoughts going through
my mind and drifted off deeply until my eyes
were completely blind. I finally reached that sink-
ing peaceful sleep; this dream felt so amazingly
true that it was one I wanted to keep. I looked over
at his wagging body and realized it was Kine, then
had a special moment, remember-ing when he
became partly mine. I knew he was that rambun-
ctious puppy in his prime. I never thought I would
see him again in this lifetime. While I was sitting
down in a restful way, I saw her figure and thought
how much I wanted to stay. She reached towards
the side of my face with her soft hand feeling so
real; I never thought it was something I would feel.
I gazed into her bright blue eyes with them saying
hello and she had a precious smile and a glorious
glow. Her sweet cheeks so peachy pink, I thought
how I did not even want to blink. Feeling her love
for me so strongly through her touch, I appreciated
this thoughtful time I had with her so much. Acknow-
ledging I was having theprivilege for the first time
of meeting this special little human being, I felt
completely shocked this was something I was seeing.
Thank you for coming to visit me, Brooklynne Grace,
I feel so blessed to have seen your beautiful face.

63

"Last night an angel of the God

to whom I belong and whom I

serve stood beside me."

Acts 27:23

Power of His Love

Many meaningless desires are being displayed
to me daily, trying to take over what I truly
believe. I know how much you love my soul
so please help me push away that dreadful pull.
I can feel it throughout my days and I just pray
I can give only you precious praise. You
deserve so much more than I can give but I
want to show you the way I should live. I
promise you that before I say a word, your
voice is what I will try to put forward. When
I feel weakness running through my veins, I
am determined to give you my heart so you
can take away these strains. You carried the
cross on your shoulders so I could move these
stressful boulders. Trying to realize you have
the perfect timing, I will write these words
given by you with passionate rhyming.

"For I know the plans I have for

you," declares the LORD,

"plans to prosper you and not

to harm you, plans to give

you hope and a future."

Jeremiah 29:11

The Lord's prayer

This, then, is how you should pray:

"Our Father in heaven,
hallowed be your name,
your kingdom come,
your will be done,
on earth as it is in heaven.
Give us today our daily
bread. And forgive us our
debts, as we also have forgiven
our debtors. And lead us not
into temptation, but deliver
us from the evil one."

Mathew 6:9-13

11299555R00044

Made in the USA
San Bernardino, CA
03 December 2018